THE LAW OF ATTRACTION MATRIX:
The Secret Science Behind
Law of Attraction Success

SOFT COVER EDITION
September 2014

By
Dr. Jill Ammon-Wexler
http://www.BuildMindPower.com

Dr. Jill Ammon-Wexler

ISBN: 978-0-9910379-3-3

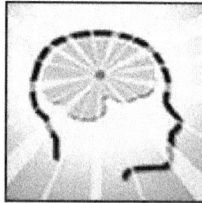

Kindle Edition Published by
Quantum Self Group, Inc.
217 Cedar Street #268,
Sandpoint, Idaho 83864 USA

TABLE OF CONTENTS

Dr. Jill Ammon-Wexler

FORWARD

You are obviously curious about the potential power of the Law of Attraction -- that's why you were attracted to this book. My intention is to take you a large step beyond curiosity straight into remarkable success with this life-transforming method of goal achievement.

How do you know if cutting through the illusions surrounding the "Law of Attraction" ... then putting the science-based version of this goal achievement method is right for you?

Should you swallow the red pill and break through to a new way of interpreting what we call "reality" and our so-called "personal limitations?" The following scenario has been included to help you decide for yourself.

Red Pill or Blue Pill?

You absolutely will not be ready for it when it comes. No one ever is. One day when you're just waiting for

Dr. Jill Ammon-Wexler

a stop light to change, you'll suddenly feel a cold wind blow right through your mind. You might look at the red light and suddenly reminder the scene from *The Matrix* when Neo decides to take the red pill and embrace certain destruction of his mental mirage.

Maybe it's a warm day and you can't imagine where "that" came from. Or maybe it's a cold day, but you still can't shake off the fact that the wind was "inside" your head. You're shocked into a strange awareness. This is your first indication of the level of challenge and change that's coming your way..

Or ... maybe you're at home and you suddenly walk into the bedroom, dig an old shark tooth hanging from a piece of leather from a dresser drawer (a remnant of your earlier hippy years) and hang it around your neck.

Or perhaps your call may come in the stillness of the night while you toss and turn, wide awake and ruminating about the predictions of coming unrest and inflation. The prospects seem to be a dreamscape.

No matter how your "call" finds you, destiny is about to seize control of your "ordinary" life. You might want to remain in your "comfort zone," even though it has suddenly become uncomfortable. You might complain that you're too old, too young, or not emotionally ready.

But some mysterious adventure is seizing your dreams, your waking life, and even your new wild visions of what could be.

The truth is, once you receive the call it's already too late to protest. Nothing can stop it and you can never really go back to your "ordinary" life. Like Neo, you already swallowed the red pill.

1. You have already "qualified"

Oprah Winfrey has something powerful to say about what you may be experiencing: *"The real work of our lives is to become aware. And awakened. To answer the call."*

You don't feel "qualified" or ready to embrace radical change? Is anyone ever ready for this? Of course not!

Underneath everything else that you call "you" is a unique, totally original and profoundly real and truly alive version of you that is bursting with potential. If you don't know why everything suddenly feels gray and boring, then your call is right on time.

2. Life may start to unravel

Once you have received your wake-up call, life may begin to slowly "come apart" around the edges. This may start so small it may seem like a flash of light just out of the corner of your eye.

You may begin to experience unusual thoughts and phenomena. You might try to brush these off, but your illusions are starting to dissolve. Your old values begin to drop into the dust and you struggle to define a new set of values. Even your "to-do" list changes.

3. You start to fly apart

"It is by going down into the abyss that we recover the treasures of life. Where you stumble, there lies your treasure." Joseph Campbell

You begin to seriously question your old reality. What was once important may now seem trivial.

Your beliefs and assumptions start to crumble. You feel less drawn to things you once valued and thought you needed.

Time starts to compress, stretch out, then compress again. Your cat still wakes you, you still start the day with a cup of coffee, you still fight the traffic to get to the office ... everything is the same and yet it is very, very different.

You no longer trust anything you once thought you knew for sure. Then one blink of an eye later...

4. The bottom drops out...

Suddenly nothing makes sense. You feel broken and hopeless.

You believe in nothing and in no one -- even your own self. You have no purpose with any meaning at all. You feel certain you're about to die in pain and emptiness.

The bottom drops out and you've lost all hope of finding any meaning to your life. You're broken and defenseless. You surrender and watch all your fears parade by. Your life looks meaningless.

5. You surrender and transform

"Am I a butterfly dreaming I am a man, or a man dreaming I am a butterfly?" Gautama Buddha

You drift into a deep dark sleep and cry out to know the purpose of your life journey. Then you hear the distant sound of bells. You follow the bells and glide formless and empty into a temple filled with light.

You notice how free you feel, no longer loaded down with worthless things from a life you no longer recognize as your own.

You realize you've left everything behind. Your identify is formless and no longer connects what you do to "make a living," where or how you live, how you dress your body or the friends you have. You are truly an empty vessel. You let go.

The caterpillar begins its transformation into a butterfly.

You are not who you thought you were. You sense excitement as you are reborn into a new vision.

"Everything changes when you start to emit your own frequency rather than absorbing the frequencies around you, when you start imprinting your intent on the universe rather than receiving an imprint from existence." Barbara Marciniak

The beating of your heart dances to the divine music of the spheres that bind the universe into one.

You're home. You begin the cycle of life anew, but with a clear vision and new sense of worth.

You choose to apply the Law of Attraction to create your new reality.

A Note From the Author

We truly live in amazingly challenging times today. Like Neo in *The Matrix* movie, our ability to survive and prosper depends on extremely clear vision and focused action.

If you are ready to "take the red pill" like Neo did and seize the opportunity to remake your personal reality, this short book is intended especially for YOU.

I sincerely hope it serves you well.

Dr. Jill Ammon-Wexler

Dr. Jill Ammon-Wexler

ONE. LOA GOAL SUCCESS

The "Law of Attraction," is often misunderstood. Contrary to popular thought, this method does *not* make things happen just because you "ask" for it.

No matter how you describe your efforts to achieve a goal, there's an art and science behind getting what you want in life that goes beyond "magic" or "luck."

In this first lesson we'll review six self-mastery insights that clarify what fuels *genuine* Law of Attraction (LOA) success.

All that is required is to wrap these tools and insights into a Self Mastery Daily Action that will get what you want to begin to *happen* in your life!

The six components of genuine, <u>brain-based</u> Law of Attraction goal success are:

1. Clarity

2. Commitment

13

3. Passion

4. Positive Emotions

5. Clear Focus

6. Daily Action

Note that creating a detailed goal planning strategy is NOT included in the above list. This is *not* an accident.

The strategy you are about to learn comes BEFORE detailed goal planning, and actually also underlies any traditional goal strategy you may later choose to use.

The techniques you are about to explore have been used by Oprah, Bill Gates, Steve Jobs of Apple Computers, Tom Watson (the founder of IBM), winning elite athletes and endless super achievers that have gone before you.

Each of the essential components of this strategy are detailed in this lesson. Approach this with an open mind, and you will find your levels of success changing in very unexpected ways.

1. CLARITY

Clarity can be defined as: "the property of being clear or transparent." Think about what this means in terms of both the Law of Attraction and traditional goal setting. "Clarity" refers to your ability to clearly visualize in your "mind's eye" something you want to have or become.

As a mentor to people that want to transform their dreams into reality, the first question I'm often asked is: "How can I be really sure I will achieve the goals I'm setting?

My answer is this: You need to start by being REALLY CLEAR about exactly what you want to achieve. You may think this is obvious, but this is a major cause of failure of Law of Attraction goal setting.

I have often found for years that many people who come to me for success training thinking they're clear about what they want are often not as clear as they thought.

Let's look at an example: A business man came to me for Law of Attraction success mentoring. (We'll call him Robert.) When I asked Robert what his goal was, he said, "I want to be financially secure ... and rich, actually." Now that's a desire most of us can relate to. But here's the problem – Robert had no idea of what his desire meant in terms of LOA success.

I asked him what the words "financially secure and "rich" meant to him. When he answered, "A lot of money," I then asked him how much money. After a few more questions Robert said he wanted to be a millionaire.

OK, that was a bit clearer. But even a million dollars is still a nebulous thing. Money is just a medium of exchange, and almost impossible to visualize. So we dug deeper to get at what Robert really wanted.

In the end we had a clear picture: He wanted a 2-story 3-bedroom house in Palm Beach, zero credit card debt, and an income of $10,000 a month to support his family and send his son to a nearby university.

Robert felt neither the Law of Attraction nor traditional goals had ever worked for him, but the real problem was that he hadn't clearly defined exactly what he wanted.

Now we had a starting point. What was Robert's solution? It became clear that his immediate initial

LOA goal should be: "To be totally confident I can actually create what I desire."

So we broke his desire for "increased financial security" down into a specific LOA goal to: (1) Increase business profit by 10%, (2) Use 75 percent of that increased profit to reduce credit card debt, and ... (3) save the remaining 25% for his son's university books and fees in the coming semester.

The key to all of this was the 10% increase in profit, so that was Robert's immediate and very specific LOA goal.

His daily goal then became to seriously watch for and act on any logical, intuitive or "accidental" insights or opportunities with the potential to increase his business profit by 10%.

Robert achieved his goal in only one month. He also got new insights into how he could even further increase his profit without even expanding his business.

Robert now knows and believes he can accomplish something he sets himself to achieve. This realization was even more important than the increased business profit!

None of this would have been possible without his decision of exactly what he really wanted, and by then taking focused action (not just dreaming.)

Ask yourself what Robert's story means to you? What do YOU want to have or become? Do you have a desire to be "financially secure." Then you need to go beyond just dreaming of having a certain amount of money.

You will have to get specific about exactly what you want to do or become, because only then can the Law of Attraction work for you.

2. COMMITMENT

The word "intention" is commonly defined as "a determination to act in a certain way." But having an intention might only implies that you "have in mind" to do something, or to bring about a desired situation or condition – it says nothing about a *commitment* to actually take action.

So ... in terms of your desire for LOA success, having an "intention" to do something might leave a huge exit door. Just intending to do or achieve something does NOT imply that you have made an actual commitment to do so. Does this make sense to you?

The Law of Attraction will work if there is a commitment on your part to take action. The second secret is to have a commitment to become or accomplish something. A COMMITMENT is a clear determination to actually achieve or have what you desire. This goes far beyond simply having an "intention."

Making a commitment says you will pay attention to the insights your brain provides, and will then actually put those insights into action.

Why is this important? Let's look at one of the classical models of goal achievement – that of "cause and effect." This model says your goal is an "effect" you wish to create, and your job is to identify and create the "cause" that will produce your desired effect – thereby reaching your goal.

This seems reasonable, right? So you might then assume that the cause of an effect would be a series of actions leading to that effect. This is the old action-reaction response of classical psychology and the scientific method.

If your immediate goal is to make a sandwich, you might then assume the cause would be the series of sandwich preparation steps. And if I were in your kitchen watching you, I might assume that your series of actions truly IS the cause of the final result – a sandwich.

But let's look at this on a deeper level.

The series of steps you took to make that sandwich were not the real cause. Your actions are actually themselves a result. The <u>real cause</u> was your DECISION to <u>have</u> the desired end result – a sandwich!

That decision occurred in the very instant you actually decided to take the actions required to make a sandwich. That might have occurred on a subconscious level – but it still was a decision.

Without that conscious or subconscious decision your sandwich would not have manifested (at least not by your own actions.) Your decision ultimately caused the whole series of actions that finally manifested as a sandwich.

Intention vs Commitment. Now we're talking about the difference between an intention and a commitment! If you truly want to be or achieve something, you have to DECIDE to actually manifest it. You have to truly COMMIT to have it "be so."

If you don't move your desire into the realm of a "COMMITMENT," your LOA goal efforts will not work for you. You have to get past dreaming or wondering if you can or cannot achieve what you want.

If you want to start your own online business, then decide to make it so. If you want a better relationship, decide to make it so. If you want a new job or career, decide to actually make it happen.

Avoid wasting energy trying to figure out if what you desire is "possible" to achieve. This only creates doubt. And your brain will then provide evidence to support your doubt, since that is apparently what you desire.

Make sure you have made a commitment, not just a wishy-washy intention to "try" something. Ever heard someone tell you about a goal and say something like, "Well, I'll give this a try and see how it goes." You can already sense their lack of commitment and expectation of failure.

When you've made a clear decision, the resources you need will come to you – sometimes in seemingly mysterious ways. But what's really happening is that your decision initiated a very specific physical reaction inside your brain.

As a result, you suddenly begin to notice things and events that might have always been there – but they are suddenly important enough to be noticed. If you think in terms of the Law of Attraction, this is IT in action – compliments of the responses of your amazing physical brain!

3. PASSION

The next thing you'll need is to build genuine passion to achieve your desired final outcome. Through the years many people have asked me why having passion for a desired LOA outcome is so very important.

It's commonly assumed that just setting a goal should be sufficient in and of itself. In some cases this might be so – IF the person setting the goal has a staff of other people with sufficient passion to achieve that goal *for* them.

Actually passion can be driven from two quite different directions:

A. You can have a passionate attraction to possess or become something, like a beautiful house you desire, or the status of being top salesman in your company.

OR ...

B. You can have a passionate desire to escape from something, like a job you detest, or a painful financial situation.

BOTH types of passion are powerful, but often the desire to escape an undesired situation or condition is more powerful.

It's easy to dream of having or being something better or more attractive – but the passionate desire to overcome pain will more often drive you to take action!

Passion in the Brain. Genuine passion is essential to get the Law of Attraction working as a positive force in your life.

Here's why: Having passion for something creates actual physical changes in your brain. This is why you tend to have such clear memories of intense events in your life, such as seeing a shocking traffic accident.

Intense emotion causes the release of natural chemicals and proteins in your brain that immediately strengthen the neural networks that store the memory of the event.

23

This is also the source of post-traumatic stress, where the memories of an extremely traumatic event "rerun" over and over in the background of your mind – and it doesn't take much to bring that painful memory roaring up to the surface to disrupt your peace of mind.

How Passion Activates the LOA. But back to passion and how it activates the Law of Attraction in your brain. You have a portion of your brain called the brain stem. This is actually the oldest portion of your brain, and it has a very basic and essential job.

Your brain stem is responsible for filtering all the incoming stimulus of everything happening around you. It's job is to immediately decide if a stimulus is important enough to immediately inform your higher brain (the limbic system and the cortex) about it.

So ... if you have *passionately* decided that you want to have a Toyota Matrix for example, this desire will be stored in your brain as important and to be paid attention to. Your brain stem will then watch for evidence of a Toyota Matrix, and you will suddenly notice them on the road and in parking lots.

This is your <u>brain</u> working to create what we call "the Law of Attraction."

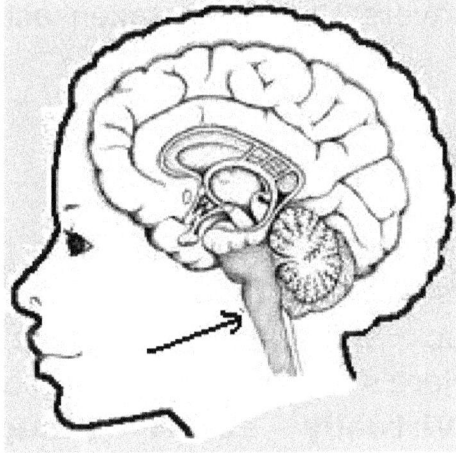

The Brain Stem

Then one day when you are at lunch with a friend you just "happen" to overhear the man at the next table tell his companion, "I've to sell my Mother's Matrix and I am ready to take any offer. She can't drive anymore."

The Law of Attraction, by way of your ever-alert brain stem, has presented the opportunity you were waiting for.

Two days later you are in your new Matrix for several thousand dollars less than the going price.

If you had not wired your brain with passion, then you would probably not even have noticed that

25

snippet of conversation, then taken action to reach your goal.

4. POSITIVE OUTLOOK

Often people sabotage their LOA goals because they do not understand the importance of maintaining a positive outlook and emotional stance about what they want. Here's why your mental outlook is so important: **Virtually EVERY thought is an intention.**

This includes every thought, including conscious, subconscious, and even the unconscious thoughts you pick up from other people.

The Impact of Worry. Worries are extremely critical, because they have negative emotional energy attached to them. This is why I say worries are negative goals. You *will* attract the *very thing you are worried about -- your brain is wired to help it manifest.*

This happens because your brain stem is designed to bring your brain's attention to every stimulus that could indicate that your worry is actually manifesting. This is how the Law of Attraction can actually attract your worries into your life!

26

Your thoughts and emotional ambience around your desired goal will either support your desire, or sabotage your efforts – there really isn't a middle ground.

Why the LOA Sometimes "Fails." Many people experience disappointment around what seems to be the "failure" of the Law of Attraction in their lives.

However the Law of Attraction has not failed. The problem is that their thoughts are in conflict. They simultaneously set the intent to achieve or become something – then turn the tables on themselves by falling into negative doubt.

This might look take the form of an inner dialogue like: "I want to start my own online business. But ... I wonder if it will work. I really have no business experience. Maybe my wife (husband, best friend, etc.) is right ... I would do better to just stick with what I'm already doing. I really don't want to waste my money or look like a fool and ... bla, bla, bla."

Or suppose you decide to lose some weight. You go on a diet and start to walk twice a day, but all the while you are thinking: "I've tried this before and it never lasts. Let's face it, I'm fat. This is hopeless."

What will happen? Your emotional ambience around your goal is negative, and probably much stronger than your positive desire. Which one do you now think will take control? Is there any doubt?

To truly achieve your desired outcome, you must clear out any negative emotions around your ability to create your desired final outcome!

You cannot allow yourself the luxury of negative thoughts around what you wish to create. True, this takes effort and practice. It's the art of learning to use your consciousness to create a congruence of positive thoughts that support your desired end result.

One great way of creating such a "congruence of positive thoughts" is to get *really clear* on what it will mean to you when you actually reach your LOA goal.

You want to clearly establish in your mind exactly how you will feel when you have reached your goal. This is very important to creating and establishing positive feelings. Begin to ask yourself what your everyday life will be like. Really go for details.

The purpose is to get in touch with the emotions connected to what you want.

5. CLEAR FOCUS

How does mental focus enter into the picture? Now we are getting to one of the most important secrets of Law of Attraction success – the undeniable BRAIN-BASED power of focused visualization of your desired goal.

Once you have determined how it will "feel" to have achieved your goal – your next job is to focus on these feelings as though your goal has *already* been achieved!

Does this sound strange, or even impossible? Actually this IS the most often missed secret of getting the Law of Attraction to work in your life.

If your desire is for more money, for example, it is important to remember that you MUST NOT just try to visualize having money – but rather visualize actively living the actual lifestyle you will live when you have achieved your goal.

Are you a hard core logical person and feel this is "ooh gum boo gum?" Then here's a couple of interesting stories you might want to think about:

Steve Jobs and Focus. Steve Jobs, the founder of Apple Computer, suffered a *dismal* failure with his first business venture. But then he turned around and successfully launched Apple out of a friend's garage.

How did this happen, and why was Jobs suddenly so successful? He told a Stanford graduating class that he suddenly had a clear, compelling, and very real detailed vision of Apples on every desk. He said the vision haunted him day and night

Many successful people use the very same tool Steve Jobs used – the creation of a clear and passionate vision, backed by committed effort.

The Power of Belief. Such visualizing of living and experiencing a successful outcome creates belief. And the power of belief is unstoppable.

Jobs described how he locked onto his vision, and vigorously committed to bring it into reality. In Jobs' own words, he became a magnet that literally drew everything he needed to him.

Tom Watson and Focus. Passionate visualization is an awesome creative force. Yet another major modern entrepreneur describes a similar process. Tom Watson, the founder of IBM, created today's billion-dollar enterprise using one simple technique –

by clearly visualizing his future success and the feelings he would experience when he achieve it.

Watson says he saw a clear picture in his mind of IBM before his company was even formed. His mental picture was as vivid and clear as the words you see here.

He said he could see the offices, the machines, the employees working busily and accomplishing their goals. He even felt the excitement of seeing satisfied customers as they shook hands with his associates.

Watson knew exactly what he was going to create. And it all began as a mental picture – a dynamically clear and detailed visualization he focused on with burning intent.

Developing LOA Focus. The point is to practice feeling the emotions attached to actually having what you want as already being in your life!

Why is this important? Because your subconscious mind absolutely does NOT know the difference between what you imagine to be true, and what is actually true!

Research has proven that when you just *imagine* lifting your arm, for example, your mind activates the same neural pathways you use when you actually raise your arm!

So really dig in to discover how it feels to have reached what you desire. Feel it, taste it, sense it, touch it – use every sense that works for you, and attach as much emotion to that sensation as possible.

Then go to work to get these feelings into your daily life. One way many people build their passion for something they wish to manifest is to create a personal "vision board" – a scrapbook or poster board upon which you have pasted pictures of your desired objects or lifestyle.

6. DAILY ACTION

There's one final and extremely important secret to getting the Law of Attraction to work in your life – commit to take consistent daily action!

Some people feel all you have to do to manifest something is to state the desire and let it go out into the universe. If this worked, everyone who ever said they wanted to be rich would BE rich. Success in any aspect of life is created one day at a time.

What sort of action am I referring to? Daily use of the proven-effective success and self mastery tools and attitudes.

These are the same tools used by Steve Jobs to create Apple Computers, Tom Watson to create IBM, and people like Mark Victor Hansen and Jack Canfield to create their mega-successful Chicken Soup empire.

It is very important to APPLY these insights on a daily basis. Why? Because SUCCESS IS CREATED ONE DAY AT A TIME, AND SO IS FAILURE! Your daily choices determine which will manifest in your life.

Dr. Jill Ammon-Wexler

TWO. THE POWER OF BELIEFS

If you have any doubt about the validity of the Law of Attraction, this will keep you from putting it to work in your life. Why? Because BELIEF is absolutely essential for the Law of Attraction (or any other type of goal-setting project) to work in your life!

The goal of this chapter is to catapult you into a new level of belief in the scientific validity of the Law of Attraction.

THE INFLUENCE OF BELIEF

For years it was assumed that the Law of Attraction was some kind of mystical or paranormal phenomenon. However recent scientific and psychological research have now shown otherwise.

I'm sure you realize that your outward actions reflect your personal beliefs. But this goes even deeper.

Your actions are actually a *direct* outward expression of your innermost beliefs!

What are beliefs? Our beliefs often seem to be a mystery, but in truth they are simply thoughts that have become deeply embedded assumptions. Note the word "assumptions." When something becomes a belief, we then assume that it is beyond question. It is then simply TRUE in our mind, and that's it!

I'm sure you've noticed how emotional you can become if someone challenges one of your beliefs. This is because a thought about something actually *becomes* a belief because of the intense emotion attached to that thought.

When intense emotion is connected to a thought or event, this causes the release of certain brain chemicals that "anchor" that thought into your brain's physical neural networks.

The more intense the emotion attached to a belief – the more impact it will have on your life. Think about that for a moment.

Suppose you "believe" you are an intelligent person with great potential. This belief will then guide your actions, and your belief will therefore create your reality.

While if you believe you are unsuccessful and doomed to failure – that will tend to manifest in your life. In effect, that will be the reality you will create in your life.

You can discover what your core beliefs are by just noticing what your actions are! Remember -- your actions directly reflect your beliefs.

Your Belief Filter. We each tend to view life through the filter of our own individual belief systems. That filter determines the quality of our choices. An important step toward Law of Attraction success is therefore to become aware of your own core beliefs.

What do YOU believe to be true about having money or financial prosperity? About having a loving relationship? About radiant health? About a promising future, regardless of what is happening around you? About your ability to spring back from a set back or natural catastrophe?

As you examine your beliefs, you'll want to challenge the truthfulness behind any beliefs that suggest you are somehow limited.

Remember: *A belief is only an emotion-charged habitual thought*. And because beliefs have a physical reality in your brain, they CAN be over-written by new, more empowering beliefs.

WHAT EINSTEIN STARTED

You probably automatically connect the name Einstein with the field of science called quantum physics – the study of reality on the subatomic (smaller than the atom) level.

One of the most interesting lessons from quantum physics is that when scientists intend to observe something (a sub-atomic particle or light photon), that "thing" changes its basic form just *because* it is being observed.

Think about what this means to YOU for a moment. You too exert a personal sub-atomic effect on the physical matter you interact with simply because of the force of your mental intention.

In terms of the Law of Attraction, this provides a solid, science-based explanation of exactly *how* our thoughts and intentions actually create what we call our "reality."

Einstein was not alone. There have since been many Nobel Laureate scientists who agree that intending to observe something actually directly affects the behavior of what is being observed.

How mind-bending is that? In other words, you will "see" (or manifest) what you intend to see. And what you intend to see is always according to your beliefs.

This is how you create your own life reality using the Law of Attraction! What you intend to observe is what the universe will create in your experience – and this is <u>always</u> in accordance with your beliefs.

An Interesting Example

Here's an interesting example of this in action: A Japanese scientist, Dr. Masaru Emoto, has a passionate interest in studying water at microscopic levels.

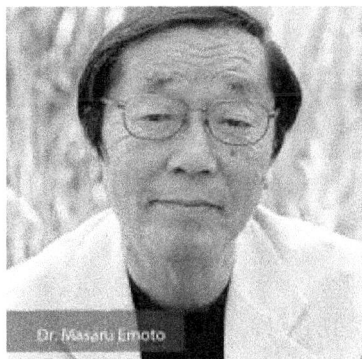

Dr. Masaru Emoto

Dr. Jill Ammon-Wexler

Emoto's photographs have shown that frozen water crystallizes differently in direct response to the conscious intention of either an individual or a group of people.

Even simply writing a different message on a bottle of water seems to dramatically change the composition of the water in the bottle.

Take a look at the below sample of Emoto's work. An intentional message of a feeling of love caused seriously polluted water to create beautiful and artistic crystals when frozen.

The below photo is water taken from the Fujiwara dam in Japan. Note the absence of any crystal-like formations in the frozen sample of this polluted water.

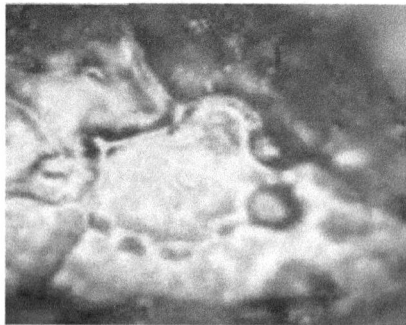

The below photo is of a frozen sample of the same water after a prayer (focused intention) for cleansing was offered. Note the ordered crystalline form of this sample.

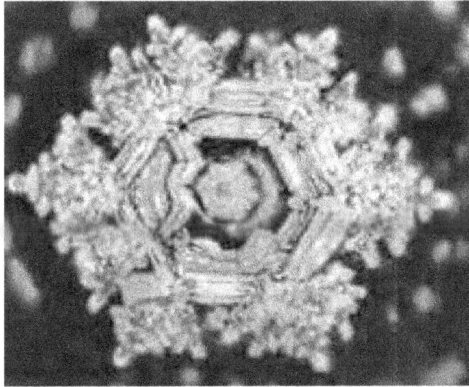

Emoto's Message. The meaning of Emoto's work is simple and profound: Your body and brain contain as much as 70% water. Emoto believes that each of our thoughts affect and change our cellular water, just as they influence the water outside our bodies.

Think about how your thoughts directly affect your body on a cellular level. Do you still have any doubt about the power of a thought to create your reality – from your very own brain cells out?

Dr. Jill Ammon-Wexler

THREE. INTENTION & AWARENESS

We have gone through all of the steps required to decide what you want and apply the Law of Attraction to attain it. But let's visit the importance and power of INTENTION in greater detail.

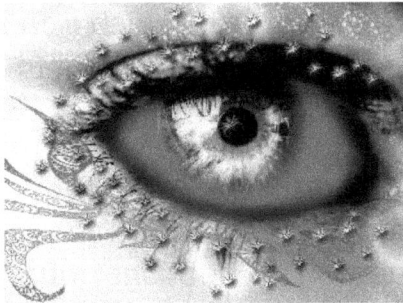

The issue of "intending" something is NOT the same as ordinary goal setting. Creating a Law of Attraction intention takes us into the realm of focused awareness and consciousness.

I am convinced from my studies of the Law of Attraction, quantum physics, shamanism and the ancient mystery schools that consciousness is the

43

"glue" that holds everything together. That gluey, sticky field then differentiates to create everything we perceive, think and feel – our awareness.

THE NATURE OF AWARENESS

Exactly what IS awareness? It is basically our ability to be conscious of something – whether an event, an object, a thought, a sensory pattern or a trend.

Awareness is trained through experience. As you grow, your awareness forms the foundation of your beliefs. Unlike thoughts, which create conscious mental images or words, your beliefs are silent and lie hidden deep in your subconscious mind.

Suppose, for example, you had a childhood experience that made you feel uncomfortable in a crowd. As an adult the subconscious belief you are unsafe in a crowd would have been programmed into your subconscious mind.

If you suddenly found yourself in a crowd, your logical mind may then try to reassure you – but your brain will have already created an intense stress response that will dominate and you will feel uncomfortable.

THE POWER OF AWARENESS

What is the power of awareness? Shifts in awareness have been shown to dramatically change lives.

A brilliant demonstration of this was provided in a 1979 experiment by Harvard psychologist Ellen Langer. Langer and her research associates managed to reverse the biological age of a group of men 75 years and older in only one week.

The men were invited to spend a week at a country retreat, and were asked <u>not</u> to bring any newspapers, magazines, or family photos taken in the past 20 years. The reason for this rather odd request became obvious when the men arrived at the resort, which had been rigged to duplicate life as it had been 20 years earlier.

Although the men were all retired, they were asked to discuss their careers as though they were presently active. Instead of current magazines, the reading tables were stocked with magazines from 20 years earlier. The music that was played was also from 20 years earlier.

The men were directed to behave as if it was 20 years earlier. All of their conversation with the other men had to refer to events and people current at that time. Each man wore an ID badge with a photo of himself from 20 years ago, and they learned to identify each other by these photos.

The Harvard team found that the men began to change remarkably. Their memory and manual dexterity improved, and they began to take more initiative in making their own meals and cleaning up after themselves.

Measurements of their finger length, which tends to become shorter during age, were also interesting. The men's fingers had lengthened during the one-week experience, the strength of their hand grip improved, and their postures had straightened and often added height. Half of the men also showed remarkably improved IQ scores.

After the study, a group of impartial judges were asked to study the before and after photos of the men. The judges reported that the men looked remarkably younger in their "after" pictures.

CONSCIOUSNESS AND AWARENESS

The nature of "consciousness" has been debated by philosophers and scientists for centuries.

Our consciousness is generally understood to refer to the relationship between our mind and the external world we interact with. It has been defined as: "The

ability to be aware of and experience feelings, wakefulness, having a sense of selfhood, or the executive control system of the mind."

Suppose we use a bright light to represent our level of consciousness or awareness: The brightness of our awareness lights up our surroundings so that we can consciously extend our physical senses and intuitive understanding into our surroundings. So you can see how Law of Attraction success depends on our level of consciousness.

Your brain expresses consciousness by producing concepts and words. Your body, on the other hand, expresses consciousness by producing molecules that carry messages initiating bodily responses.

But quantum physics tells us there's little difference between a thought and a molecule. Here's an example of how your thoughts and your body's molecules meld together to create a response to life:

Consider what happens when you bite into a fresh lemon. The lemon juice instantly stimulates your salivary glands and this makes your mouth "water."

47

What's really happening is that the salivary glands have been stimulated to release important digestive enzymes – salivary amylase and salivary maltase.

Take a moment to do a little experiment. Just say the word lemon out loud four or five times. Did you notice that your mouth began to "water." Your salivary glands are producing enzymes, even though there's no lemon present.

It seems that the message created and sent from your brain is more important that the actual presence of food.

This is a prime example of how words alone can trigger an actual physical reaction. Your thought of a lemon was not a "thing" – yet your body tried to "digest" your word.

HOW can only the word "lemon" and a mental picture of a lemon create the this result? This is a direct example of the power of a simple word to directly influence you on an undeniable physical level. In short, a word just transformed your reality.

Dr. Jill Ammon-Wexler

FOUR. THE POWER OF WORDS

Probably you recall a parent or a teacher saying you were "smart," or "special" or "pretty." Even the memory of such an event can trigger a warm glow in your heart and mind.

Actually words alone make (and can change) your life. So ... can a simple verbal message actually change your intelligence? Yes! Here's an example of this in action:

It's just after "reading time" in a Los Angeles second grade classroom. The attractive brunette teacher inserts a bookmark, closes her worn copy of "Alice in Wonderland," and gently placed the book on her desk. As always after storytelling, her 23 young charges were attentive – waiting for their teacher's "story questions."

"What color do you think Alice's eyes were?" she asked the class.

51

Arms shot up. The rapid-fire answers spanned every possible eye color – from blue to green to brown to black.

"Actually," she said, holding up the book, "you can see on the cover that Alice's eyes are blue. And here's what's so interesting about that. You know from the story that Alice is very curious and likes adventure. Right?"

Chirps of agreement come from the class.

"Well," she continued, "since Alice's eyes are blue, we know something very special about her." Keeping her agreement with a friend who is doing a psychology study, she then recited a script the psychologist provided: "Scientists did research that proved blue-eyed children are a lot smarter than brown- or green-eyed children. Isn't that interesting? So if you have blue eyes you are naturally smarter, just like Alice."

Do you remember how you trusted and admired your teachers as a young child? The students believed their teacher, of course.

The results were immediate and dramatic. The blue-eyed children immediately began to outperform their brown- and green-eyed classmates in all aspects of their studies.

The improvements continued until, one month later, the teacher announced that she had made a mistake. She apologized, and says the study actually proved that brown- and green-eyed children are the most intelligent.

Again the results were dramatic and immediate. The blue-eyed children lost their edge and their performance dropped. The brown- and green-eyed children's grades, on the other hand, immediately soared to the superior range.

Incidentally, at the end of the test period the teacher did tell her students that the scientists were totally wrong – that eye color is not an indicator of intelligence. The children's performance then quickly returned to pre-experiment levels, regardless of their eye color.

Words and Consciousness. The words we use, determine who we become. What does that experiment with the school children prove?

If you tell yourself that you're smart, you'll act (and become) smart. If you tell yourself that you're creative, you'll act (and become) creative. If you tell yourself that you're a success, you'll act (and become) successful. If you tell yourself that you're excellent, you'll act (and become) excellent. If you tell yourself that you can achieve higher levels of consciousness, you'll act and become more aware on a conscious level.

Considering the results of that study, it seems clear that our ability to make our lives whatever we wish them to be depends on what we believe! If you tell yourself something is beyond your control, then it truly will be beyond your control. While if you believe and consistently tell yourself you can change it, then you can!

WORDS & FOCUSED AWARENESS

Let's cut to a practical way to achieve higher levels of awareness and consciousness. Your thoughts and words create the platform for your personal potential – including your ability to manifest your Law of Attraction goals.

That old saying, "you become what you think about" is more than just a saying. Your mental focus actually creates your brain-based reality. And your words are a direct expression of that focus.

Picture a foot path through a meadow. Walking over the path every day creates a clear, well-defined path. But if you don't walk on the path, it will eventually grow over and disappear.

So the more often you use a certain word "about" your Law of Attraction goal, the more the neural pathways connected to that word will gain strength. Does this seem too simple?

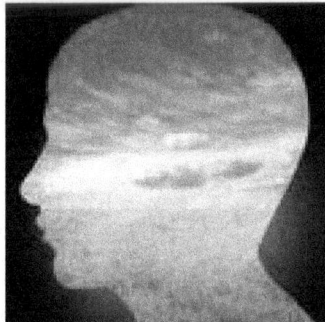

Your brain loves habit. Just like the path through that meadow, the cell-to-cell pathways in your brain are "worn in" (strengthened) by frequent use. Here's how that works:

So here's why we really are "what we tell ourselves we are:" The more consciously (or subconsciously) you use certain words to describe yourself and your

LOA goal, the stronger the associated brain pathways become.

It really is that simple. What you "tell" yourself with your words will grow stronger! This is not theory – it's the proven scientific reality of how your brain works.

WORDS CREATE YOUR REALITY

In terms of achieving your Law of Attraction goal, the language you use to refer to your progress is critically important. Your mind-body system organizes itself around verbal experiences.

Your body operates from a constant network of messages flowing through it. Some of these messages sustain and nourish you on a physical and mental level – while others may lead to undesired states and limitations.

Medical research has established that nurturing is valuable both mentally and physiologically! If a newborn child is spoken to, touched and caressed – their level of human growth hormone increases and the protective coating (myelin) over their motor nerves becomes thicker.

The mother's urge to cuddle and speak to her child directly converts into a life-sustaining *biochemical* reaction.

We literally create our reality and our lives out of words.

Dr. Jill Ammon-Wexler

FIVE. THE POWER OF INTENTION

This brings us to the concept of intention – the primary topic of this chapter. Webster's dictionary includes a useful definition of intention: "A stretching or bending of the mind toward an object ... fixedness of attention; earnestness."

When you have an intention to manifest a Law of Attraction goal, there's an underlying implication of intense belief, determination and resolve. This goes far beyond "ordinary" goal setting.

While ordinary goal setting implies a certain level of desire to attain an end result – a Law of Attraction intention to reach that goal implies a burning and unwavering determination. In short, it is a stretching of your mind's awareness and consciousness toward that goal.

This is quite different from "trying" to reach a certain goal. The word "try" implies the possibility of failing to reach the goal – while an intention does not recognize the possibility of failure.

BENDING YOUR MIND

Learning to apply intention to control outcomes is a shared goal of several spiritual traditions. In India, the esoteric practice of Tantra teaches very elaborate practices and exercises designed to teach the student to control their so-called "involuntary" physiological responses.

Young Tibetan Buddhist monks are fully expected to demonstrate their ability to intentionally control their bodily responses by being able to sit on a frozen patch of land and mentally melt the ice around them.

Native American Indians, Canadian First Nation's peoples and shamanic cultures around the world have practices that all call upon exercising the same power using one's focused intent.

What is the source of this intentional power? It all begins with exercising conscious awareness. In fact, this is the VERY same "bending of the mind" that

WILL occur when you begin to assert control over any of your bodily functions.

A MIND BENDING EXERCISE

Try the following exercise for your own direct experience of intention-based mind bending: Grasp something weighing from 2- to 5-pounds in one of your hands. If you don't have any weights, just put a couple of 16-ounce cans of soda in a plastic bag and grasp the handles of the bag).

Relax your arm and have a friend move your weighted arm up and down about 20 times to "exercise" your biceps. (Make NO active effort on your part). Having your arm moved in this way obviously does not involve any active intentional awareness or behavior on your part.

Next have a friend step back while you use your personal intention to slowly lift the weighted bag as you flex your bicep. Really focus your awareness on your bicep, and feel it contract as you lift the bag.

What did you just experience? As you actively engaged in lifting the weight, signals were being sent to your brain's motor cortex. Interestingly, research has established that as you do this your heart and

61

lung tissues, immune system, endocrine glands, and the areas of your brain controlling motor coordination are all stimulated by your conscious and intentional behavior.

Your holistic mind-body system reacts to such an intentional action in a holistic manner. In effect, stimulating your bicep muscle actually transferred into your entire being on both mental and physical levels. In you think of your being in quantum terms, you caused a shift in your entire quantum field.

APPLYING INTENTION

Suppose you have a deep desire to move to Hawaii and live a simple life. But on a conscious level you "know" this is not realistic because bla...bla...bla...

How can you override the fact that your conscious mind is killing your goal? You are going to have to make a decision to intend to "make it so."

Here is where the traditional cause-effect goal model must be replaced with an intention-based Law of Attraction goal model. It does NOT matter if you consciously feel it is "impossible" to manifest your goal. (With your old way of cause-effect thinking, it probably IS impossible.)

And it does NOT matter if you cannot clearly see exactly HOW you will manifest your goal. How can that be? Because everything will begin to take place AFTER you've set your intention, but NOT before.

The first step in getting something you don't have today is to convert your desire into a Law of Attraction INTENTION. This is NOT the same as thinking about whether or not you can achieve it! This is about setting an intention to HAVE it.

Want to change careers? Then create an intention to do so. Want to move? Just decide and intend to do so. Want a better relationship? Really decide and intend to get it. When you want to create a new outcome -- first take the time to become clear about what you want, then just DECIDE to create an unwavering intention to have it.

Is your desired outcome possible? Here's how this works: If you cannot clearly see yourself achieving that goal, your mind will probably provide steady evidence that the goal is impossible. But if you simply set an intention without being concerned about "HOW," then such objections dissolve.

On the other hand, think about "trying" and you'll set yourself up to accept failure. Have you ever heard someone mention one of their goals, but you could sense that they were uncertain and uncommitted? Perhaps they shared a clue like, "I'm going to try to get a new job." What does the word "try" say? It says lack of commitment and belief.

SOME PRACTICAL REMINDERS

Be Clear. When you intend to create something new in your life, you may at first see no results at all. General intentions have very little power. Set laser-clear intentions and you'll get there much faster.

Avoid setting an intention because you feel you *should* want something. Be honest with yourself and focus on what YOU really want. Setting an intention that does not match your innermost values will set you at odds with yourself. This will only create internal conflict.

Watch Your Thoughts. Virtually every thought has the potential power of an intention. Your job is to identify and eliminate any thoughts conflicting with your desired intention. You cannot hold a thought like, "I hate being depressed" while intending to be happy. "I hate being depressed" sets an internal belief that you ARE depressed.

So ... avoid acknowledging what you don't want. To do so will simply glue it into your life. You do not have to engage in "denial+ -- actually the opposite. Just defocus your mind from what you don't want, and shift your focus on what you do what.

Watch Your Words. As you know, the words you use to describe your progress on the way to achieving your intention are very important. Build your awareness of what you are saying to yourself. Convert any negative or limiting words to represent a more optimistic outlook!

Avoid Belief-Conflicts. If you set an intention that flies in the face of your beliefs – you are setting yourself up for failure. This would be like holding the intention to become a multi-millionaire when your mind is loaded with limiting beliefs about having abundance in your life. If you try to hold an intention conflicting with your dominant beliefs, that intention is doomed to fail.

If you are determined to set an intention that flies in the face of strong negative beliefs, you have two options: First work on reprogramming or replacing those beliefs, OR work "around the edges" of your major intention. Set an ongoing series of related intentions, with each one just a little beyond your comfort zone. Then stretch yourself a bit further!

Stay Focused. If you catch yourself engaging in mental laziness or negative thinking, just turn your attention back to what you want. With practice you'll find it easier to stay focused on your desires without such internal resistance.

Persist. Perhaps the #1 reason people fail to manifest an intention is a lack of persistence. To realize your intention more readily, take a few minutes to focus on your intentions at least twice a day. If you find yourself with nothing to do, mentally focus your thoughts onto actually living your intention.

SIX. THOUGHTS AS ENERGY

Let's take another quick look at quantum physics. It is now widely accepted among quantum scientists that virtually everything is energy in motion.

Your automobile, the walls of your office, your desk, the clothing on your body, your body itself – it's all vibrating energy on the most basic level.

Each of your thoughts are also energy, and can be observed using today's high tech equipment as they pass through your brain.

You can compare a thought to a spark that rises from a campfire. For although your thoughts contain the essence and potential power of the fire – they exist for only seconds, then simply dissipate.

Because a thought lasts only from two to three seconds, you might assume thoughts don't have much power. But this is where the power of focus and repetition come into play.

A thought that is repeated with intense focus becomes concentrated mental power – just as sunlight can create fire when focused through a magnifying glass.

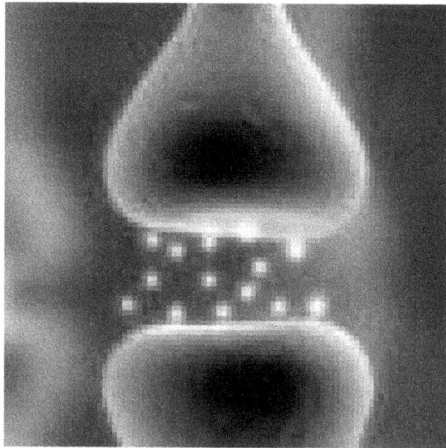

The signal connection between neurons

The more often a focused thought is repeated, the more energy and power it can generate. This is not theory – it is based on the fact that a single thought activates hundreds (and even thousands) of new neural connections in our brain.

Then if that thought has intense emotion attached to it, a cellular reaction occurs that "cement" a memory of that thought in place. This is why it's so easy to remember an emotional-charged event.

The old belief about the Law of Attraction was that we somehow "magically" attract circumstances matching our thought images. But there's a science-based way to interpret this phenomenon.

Here's how that works: Any well-focused, emotion-charged thought that is repeated generates powerful neural pathways of the desired reality in your physical brain – and this enables your subconscious mind to direct your actions in order to create your desired reality.

Furthermore, since your subconscious mind operates 24/7 (even when you're sleeping), it is constantly ready to notice anything that reminds it of your focused thought, or desire.

If you bought a new red Toyota RAV4, for example, you would suddenly notice every red RAV4 you pass on the highway or see in the parking lot.

They were always there – it's just that your excitement over your new RAV4 has primed your subconscious mind to notice anything related to your new RAV4.

MODERN SCIENTIFIC VIEWS

Until recently our most common scientific theories were based on Isaac Newton's 300 year-old theory of a universe in which all matter moved around within three dimensional space and time according to fixed laws.

But today's scientific discoveries have created a radically different view of our reality. We've already discussed how quantum physics shows that your intent to observe something actually influences sub-atomic reality to "create" that something.

Now the scientific discipline known as "Field Theory" has added yet another dimension to this. Modern Field Theory proposes that ALL of life exists as a single part that affects the whole at every moment.

So while the old scientific theories told us we were separate from the rest of life – Field Theory suggests a very different view of what is "in here" and "out there."

According to Field Theory, we ARE our world. What we call "reality" is not fixed, but is changeable and open to influence – and the highly organized energy of consciousness (or mind) has the ability to change anything and everything.

Field Theory also proposes that both time and space are actually an ever present "now" and "here." A great deal of new scientific research evidence has now shown that any focused "intention" actually travels across time and space.

Experiments have been done to study the effect that mind has on physical matter. It has been clearly demonstrated that mind DOES affect and change physical matter.

AND it has also been demonstrated that this occurs no matter when an intention to change something is generated, or how far away the person (the source of the intent) is from the target physical object.

Based on their experiments, Field Theory scientists now tell us that the future is constantly acting on the present.

When an action involving intent is analyzed, there appears to be a "backward flow" from the "future" result to the "past" cause, or moment of intention.

This finding brings us to a remarkable conclusion: Setting an "intention" to have or do something may not initiate something running forward in time. Setting that intention to may rather be an "information flow" that moves to us "backward" from our future to the present.

This suggests that our future actions, choices and possibilities actually create our present intentions.

Can you handle what this means? This implies that you have actually ALREADY achieved your Law of Attraction goal, and that your current intention to reach toward it has come backward to you through time.

Think of the implications of this: Every action you take or thought you have in the present may have come backward to you from the future. A strange concept indeed.

And if truly everything is everywhere at once, perhaps there is NO end or beginning to anything ... and you truly ARE already living in the future reality that you are NOW bringing into being.

The important point to realize is this: The passionate thing you want to create already IS, and your intent to create it is pulling you forward from the future. You WILL reach your passionate Law of Attraction goal, because you already HAVE reached it.

This underscores the importance of going after a project that burns inside of you passionately ... of listening to the yearnings of your inner self and its very real connection to your future self.

Dr. Jill Ammon-Wexler

SEVEN. YOUR ACTION PLAN

If we relate to our lives within the context of Quantum Physics, Field Theory, and how the brain works – it becomes obvious that we truly DO create our lives by consciously or unconsciously choosing from among the many options available to us.

Think for a moment what this means to your life: You create your personal reality with each choice you make, and what you commit to. And you constantly alter your reality by your choices and power of focus.

The things you do NOT choose remain only a potential reality, and essentially become invisible to you. But this "potential reality" is always available IF you CHOOSE to master the skills required to be aware of all the options available to you. You can then make the most empowering choice.

Taking an LOA leap forward is simply a matter of choosing to change your focus to something new, and then passionately and totally committing to that desired new reality.

LAW OF ATTRACTION ACTION PLAN

So ... now let's put all of this together to describe a science-based Law of Attraction goal-attainment formula, and see how you can put it to work in your life.

Any true LOA goal-achievement formula must include certain basic steps: (1) Decide, (2) Commit, (3) Believe, (4) Write it, (5) Create a Daily Practice, (6) Act As If, and (7) Take Action and Pay Attention. Each of these has science-based foundations that have already been explained in the previous pages.

STEP 1: DECIDE. One single thing stands out as the most important start of any Law of Attraction project – a clear vision of exactly what you want. Many take the importance of this for granted – assuming they have a clear vision, when all they have is desire and wishing.

Napoleon Hill in *"Think and Grow Rich"* says this about stepping onto the path to accumulating riches:

"The starting point is having a definite purpose backed by burning desire for its fulfillment."

What's this all about? You can only have a definite purpose IF you decide exactly what you want. And THIS is where the Law of Attraction fails for most people.

Do This Now. Do YOU know exactly what you want to become or have in your life? If not, the first step is to DECIDE exactly what it is that you want. That process has core importance.

For example: Just wanting to be rich is NOT a definite purpose. Whereas wanting $350,000 to buy a house on the canal at California's Clear Lake so you can retire there IS a definite purpose!

In making your "What I want" decisions, remember to look within yourself for what you most passionately desire – because the intense emotion created by a passionate desire is perhaps the most important KEY to Law of Attraction success!

Not only will it put your brain to work in the right way, but it increases the likelihood you are responding to a "future" reality that is pulling you toward itself (remember Field theory?)

Do Not Know Yet? If you do NOT know what you want yet, consider this: All of life seems to have an inherent creative urge to grow and develop. Your decision to study this course is part of that urge, and is moving you along on the path to self-actualization and fulfillment.

You may only know that you feel compelled to make a change, to expand, to do something different. You may not be totally clear about what you want at first. That's not uncommon. If that's the case, just focus on listening to your deeper emotional self and see what comes up.

Just do your best and play with the following question: What do you passionately wish to become, or to have in your life?

STEP 2. COMMIT

Once you decide what you want, the next step is to make a passionate commitment to actually HAVE it in your life. Remember about the Field? It may well be that you have already achieved this in the future, and it is reaching backward to you to create your current desire and intention!

Forget the How. At first do NOT be concerned about HOW you will achieve your desire. Focus on your desired end result, not on how you will get there.

Remember how your brain works? The ways and means will show up as your brain goes to work to help you focus on opportunities related to your desire. The time for taking goal-directed action will come.

Forget What You Do Not Want. Be sure to also forget about what you do *NOT* want.

Suppose for example you want $100,000 so you can pay off all your credit card debt and start a savings account to send your son to the university. You will want to focus on HAVING the $100,000 – not on the pressure of the credit card debt and "how" to finance a college education.

Remember this: Worry is actually a very powerful form of goal setting that is backed by the power of intense emotion. Do NOT allow yourself to get caught up in worry, while ignoring focus on what you WANT.

STEP 3. BELIEVE. Remember the discussion about belief? Belief is a very powerful force that, in the end, totally determines what you will (and will not) achieve in your life.

That is one of the reasons you should NOT be concerned at first about how you will achieve what you wish to achieve. Do NOT bother yourself with the "how" in the beginning.

You have learned that the Law of Attraction is real and science-based. It IS! Just allow yourself to release doubt and explore the power of belief.

STEP 4. WRITE. Law of Attraction master teacher Napoleon Hill recommends you write a clear, concise description of exactly what you want, and THEN read it aloud twice a day.

The physical acts of writing and speaking each engage specific and very important parts of your brain. This will help create the strong neural tracks that will burn your desire into your brain. This is far more powerful than just "dreaming" of your desire!

STEP 5. DAILY PRACTICE. A belief is just a thinking habit. One excellent way to create a NEW belief is to focus on creating new habits by committing to a DAILY Law of Attraction Self Mastery practice. This makes actual physical changes in your brain.

The two ways to develop a new pattern of thought (habit) are repetition and emotion. The more emotion behind your vision of what you want, the more your brain will pay attention to your vision.

Plus the more repetition, the more likely your brain will create strong, durable neural networks that hold your vision.

A daily practice should focus on FEELING that you have already achieved your goal. Read your vision aloud, read inspiring materials, and focus on acting as if you already are the person your goal belongs to!

STEP 6. ACT AS IF

Preparing yourself to receive what you want is a critical step. Think of the way a TV receives a channel by tuning into the broadcast frequency of the channel. You can tune yourself into the "frequency" of the person your Law of Attraction goal belongs to by acting AS IF you have already achieved your goal.

Basically two steps are required to act as if:

1. Hold a clear image of your dream in your mind, and then,

2. "Act as if" it is already true.

This is a powerful and transformational self mastery tool. Whether you want to become more out-going, quit smoking, achieve a goal, or create a fulfilling relationship - the process is the same.

Just picture it in your mind, then "act as if" you have already achieved your desired goal. There are three interesting brain mechanisms behind the power of acting as if:

First, your powerful subconscious mind is NOT able to logically question what you present to it! That portion of your mind always accepts your "acting" as the literal truth.

Second, each time you act "as if" you are courageous in the face of fear, for example, your physical brain responds by building powerful and complex neural networks to support that "acting."

Third, as you repeat your "acting," those neural networks build stronger and stronger connections. As these networks increase, your "acting as if" will gain strength as an actual BELIEF.

Your reality is actually your own creation! It is simply the net outcome of the continuous stream of thoughts, emotions and images passing through your mind.

Everything you have in your life actually began as a thought. And so, changing your life must logically begin with your thoughts. Your future is actually created by your current thoughts. That's the meaning of that old saying: "Whatever you believe will become your reality."

And that brings us back around the circle to "beliefs." By acting "as if" you do not fear something, you'll be more willing to try new challenges. You will gradually become more and more fearless. Soon you will just automatically believe yourself to be fearless.

"Acting as if" you are already successful builds the expectation you will BE successful. This expectation then strengthens into a solid core belief that will guide your external behavior in appropriate ways.

"Acting as if" builds the mind power of success. And since others respond to our actions, act successful and you will be seen as successful. And that will even further strengthen your belief.

Once you are clear on your desire, your "acting as if" will create actions that will move you toward your Law of Attraction goal. Along the way watch for and pay attention to people and events that seem "coincidental" or "synchronistic." This is actually your brain working to bring such events and people to your attention.

WATCH IT HAPPEN

Accept what happens as more than just coincidental – it's a sign that your Law of Attraction goal efforts are at work in your life. Apply this to the findings of Field Theory, and you may well assume that such events are NOT unrelated at all – but are your own creation.

Grab opportunities that seem to just crop up and take a good look at them. If you meet someone who somehow mentions something related to what you are seeking, follow that clue. If you feel the urge to make a phone call or go somewhere, do it.

Pay Attention to Your Dreams. If you have always had a dream of something, there are some interesting ways to interpret your dream.

A quantum physics interpretation could be that your dream is one of your alternate realities, and that it will manifest in your life if you to choose to   it. Field Theory might say that this is your future reaching back to you, waiting for the moment of INTENT that will kick it all into place and sweep you into your future.

Either interpretation calls for the same thing – a DECISION AND INTENTION on your part – a personal commitment to "see" something occur in your life.

Use these steps to power up the science-based Law of Attraction in your life and make it easier!

Dr. Jill Ammon-Wexler

EIGHT. LOA IN YOUR BRAIN

Ever wonder why some people have such powerful luck, and seem to achieve their Law or Attraction goals so easily? Actually there's a very simple explanation for the unusual "luck" some people have – it's simply their brain following their instructions.

Your brain contains literally billions of nerve cells called neurons. Your neurons communicate with one another, creating networks of communicating neurons called "neural networks."

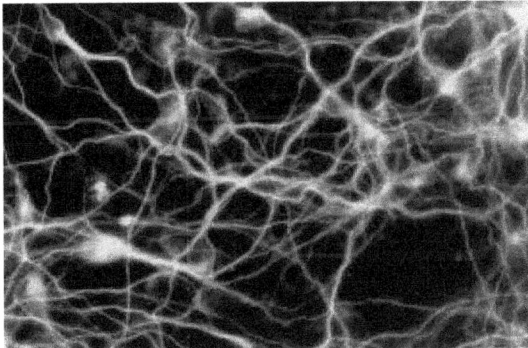

Artist's concept of a neural net

Dr. Jill Ammon-Wexler

Let's dig into your amazing brain to explore how it works. Your 3-pound brain has many different functional parts that contribute directly to your ability to manifest your desires.

The following pages explain what happens in your brain when you commit to a Law of Attraction project.

PARTS OF THE BRAIN

Your brain can be divided into many parts. But for our purposes, let's consider three major "functional" parts:

The first, oldest part of your brain is the Brain Stem that connects your brain to your spinal cord. We showed you an illustration of that earlier in the book.

The large middle part is your brain's emotional center (the Limbic System). And the thin part stretched over the outer perimeter of your brain like a swimming cap is the analytical part of your brain -- your Cortex.

THE LIMBIC SYSTEM

You're surely aware of the analytical functions of your brain provided by your Cortex, so let's jump right in and take a look at a more mysterious part of your brain – the central core commonly known as the Limbic System.

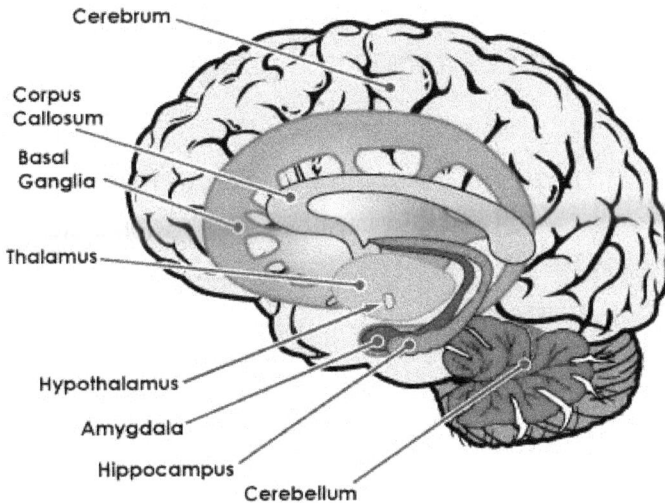

Cerebrum

Corpus Callosum

Basal Ganglia

Thalamus

Hypothalamus

Amygdala

Hippocampus

Cerebellum

Your brain's central Limbic System has a tremendous amount of influence over your ability to achieve (or fail to achieve) the end results you desire.

A small part of your brain's Limbic System called the amygdala (ah-mig-da-la) is of special interest to us. You have two amygdala – one on each side of your brain, and their basic job is to assign an emotional meaning to what you perceive (see, hear, touch, smell, etc.).

For example: If your amygdala receive a sensation of something that is somehow connected to a past negative emotion, they may serve as a "panic button" to warn you that (based on your past experience) you face a potentially dangerous situation.

But your amygdala also play a very important part in manifesting what you want. To understand this we must move down into the lower, older portion of the brain – the Brain Stem.

YOUR BRAIN'S REALITY FILTER

Your Brain Stem is the funnel that carries information from your upper brain down into your nervous system, and also carries messages up from your body to the brain.

But it has another very important job that is focused on your survival, and is critically important to Law of Attraction success.

Everything you sense (hear, see, touch, etc.) is immediately sent to your Brain Stem, and actually reaches the Brain Stem *before* it reaches the higher parts of your brain.

The instant such sensory information arrives, it is filtered by part of your Brain Stem called the Reticular Activating System, or RAS.

The job of the RAS is to quickly determine if a piece of sensory information is IMPORTANT to your survival. If it seems important, it's immediately sent up to your Limbic System where an emotional component is attached, and then to your Cortex for appropriate action.

On one level the RAS is a "negativity magnet" that constantly scans for things that are urgent or threatening. It looks for any stimulus that reminds it of something that hurt or threatened you in the past. So if you have an old "hurt" related to rejection, your RAS will be on the alert for anything that could signal possible rejection – and will send those straight up to your higher brain centers.

Your amygdala, in turn, would then automatically attach a sad or painful emotional component to any stimulus that reminds you of rejection. This is a "double whammy" that tends to keep you super sensitive to the old "stuff" in your life.

Dr. Jill Ammon-Wexler

FOCUSING YOUR BRAIN

All that might seem rather negative, but there's a way to get your brain focused on what you WANT – rather that constantly focusing only on survival and past negative experiences.

How can that happen? You're going to have to "re-focus" your amygdala and RAS toward the "sunny side of the street."

Here's how: Your RAS responds to HABITS of thought. The trick is to rewire the instructions to your RAS and amygdala to pay attention to what <u>YOU</u> feel is critical to your survival – accomplishing your LOA goal.

This calls for using your higher brain center – your analytical Cortex – to use DAILY positive focused intent and emotion to improve how your brain interprets reality.

It's the emotional content of past negative events that makes them so "solid" and fixed in your subconscious mind. The only way to fight negative emotion is with focused positive emotional intent.

Among our most powerful emotions are fear and anger. Suppose for a moment you have arrived at a point in your life that you are so afraid you will continue to be ruled by your past pain, that you become outraged and furious (super anger).

You can then be sure your RAS and amygdala will definitely pay attention, and will try to steer you away from responding to your old past pain – a 180 degree shift.

This is how something that seems negative can become super positive! But you do NOT have to start with fear and anger. Focused passionate desire has the same effect.

Dr. Jill Ammon-Wexler

NINE. THE POSITIVE SIDE OF FAILURE

This chapter focuses on why Law of Attraction efforts might sometimes seem to backfire. It also explains EXACTLY how to avoid the painful disappointment most people call "failure."

There's an old saying that's appropriate: "When one door closes, another opens." As you apply this way of viewing success and failure in your life, you may find so-called failures will truly open new doors.

Why do I say this? Because in choosing to read this book you opened yourself to create positive change in your life. In doing so you are already doing what so many people fear – shaking things up to create a NEW reality.

Part of this is based on your belief that life can be better and more fulfilling if you open yourself to new ways of thinking. Yes, it is true that this often involves a certain level of risk-taking. And risk-taking can lead to what many people call "failure."

But failure has an entirely different meaning to individuals like yourself – to those who are actively seeking to make a REAL difference in their own life. Read on to discover a new way of looking at what most people call "failure."

WHAT IS FAILURE?

Webster's dictionary defines failure as "the state or condition of not meeting a desirable or intended objective."

Most people assume that failure is the opposite of success. But this is absolutely NOT true. In terms of the science of Law of Attraction success, failure is an absolutely essential experience. Failure actually paves the road to success.

Whether we like it or not, life often brings unexpected events and outcomes. There will continue to be challenges at every stage of your life, and dealing with them positively is what success is all about.

If you are a success-seeker, failure is a reality you have to face frequently on your path to creating success.

DEALING WITH A FAILURE

There are basically three common strategies people use to deal with a "failure" event:

1. Give up and quit,

2. Try the same thing even harder, or

3. Analyze, adjust, then try again.

Let's take a closer look at each of these strategies, and give YOU a chance to think about which you tend to use.

1. Finally Give Up and Quit. Obviously the easiest response to failure is to just give up and forget what you were trying to achieve. Unfortunately this is one of the most common responses to a so-called "failure."

There's not much to say about this strategy. Maybe the goal was not right for you and abandoning it was the right thing to do. But simply giving up your goal at the first bump in the road is something entirely different.

Here's something to remember: When you fail at something, this does NOT make YOU a failure. It simply indicates that the strategy you were using did not produce the desired end result!

2. Try the Same Thing Harder. When many Law of Attraction goal seekers decide not to simply give up and quit, the next common strategy is to try the same thing harder -- often using the same approach that just failed. So what does this strategy yield? Often just more of the same, plus exhaustion and burn-out!

Albert Einstein defined crazy as, "Doing the same thing over and over again, while hoping to get different results."

3. Adapt, Adjust and Change. Here's a fact: You need to be willing to fail and adapt on your way to achieving what you want. If you give up, you waste all of the effort you have already invested. And just trying harder at an approach that fails makes no sense at all.

A good first step is to begin to interpret any failures as feedback. Don't treat failure as something bad. It simply indicates what does not work, and can shine a light on something important about why you are not getting the results you desire.

Be flexible enough to LOOK at your failures, analyze them, and learn from them. Analyze any failure as deeply as you can, then use what you have learned in creating your next strategy.

RESPONDING VS. REACTING

Life does not just "happen" to us. It's how we interpret the events around us that creates our life reality. Think about that for a moment.

Suppose you were laid off from your job. It's obvious you did NOT create the economic problems leading to that event. But you ARE in total control of how you react or respond to your "failure" to keep your job.

Here are the three choices you normally have when facing a serious challenge:

- You can REACT by getting anxious, sink into depression, and just give up. This will obviously create a negative reality in your life that could be seen as a failure.

- You can REACT by getting really angry or depressed, and then vent your anger at people around you, or just hold it inside as depression.

99

- You can instead consciously choose to RESPOND, and use your focus and energy to take action to create a positive answer.

Understanding the Difference. There's a huge difference between reacting and responding. REACTING is a "knee jerk" action controlled by the oldest, non-logical portion of our brain – the brain stem. Such reactions are usually fed by the emotions that rise up from our feelings about what happened.

RESPONDING, on the other hand, occurs in the higher thinking centers of your brain, which then sends signals down to your emotional brain so it can immediately take control of any resulting stress or fear.

Here is an important point to remember: A project failure does <u>not</u> make YOU "a failure!" It's your REACTION OR RESPONSE to what occurs that creates your personal reality!

Create a Response-Driven Life. For the most part we eat, sleep, work, play, laugh, worry, hope, plan, love, hate, cook, drive, work out – all with little consideration of whether we are reacting or responding,

This is not necessarily bad. If we gave conscious attention to every single thought or action, we would overload our brain with unimportant decisions. STILL -- Your thoughts, reactions and responses got you where you are today. And they will continue to create your future.

Your life is a mirror reflection of exactly how and what you think. Success does NOT just happen. You create it by responding to challenges along the way, OR you just give up and accept what life happens to throw your way.

Do you want more Law of Attraction success? One very important place to start is by building a success-focused habit to RESPOND to any challenges you face, instead of allowing yourself to just automatically react.

RESPONDING TO FAILURE

A major thing that separates successful people from everyone else is how they respond to failure. This is one of the prime differences between Law of Attraction winners, and those who never seem to get what they want

As explained earlier, when you hit a bump in the road on your way to a goal, you have three choices:

1. Start giving lots of excuses and give up, or

2. Just keep on doing the same thing, but try harder, or

3. See your failure as valuable feedback, learn from it, refine your strategy, and press on.

Successful people understand that failure is just feedback. They learn from that feedback and try something new. Then if they still don't achieve their goal, they get more feedback, change their strategy, and take action again. They keep repeating this process until they get what they want.

This strategy WILL enable you to achieve any goal you truly desire. And it is basically a CHOICE to adopt this attitude.

TEN. BUILD YOUR RESILIENCE

You want to be successful, so realize you WILL have to handle some failures along the way And not just handle them – but USE them constructively!

Have you ever wondered why some people seem to remain calm in the face of failure and even disaster – while others just seem to fall apart? There's a special secret to their amazing recovery power.

The people who manage to keep their cool in this way have a personal trait called resilience – a refined ability to handle problems and setbacks very effectively.

ADVANTAGES OF RESILIENCE

The dictionary defines resilience as "the positive capacity of people to cope with stress and catastrophe." And it is also used to indicate "a personal resistance to future negative events."

Those who lack resilience tend to feel overwhelmed by failures, are slower to recover, and may even experience deep emotional distress. While those who are resilient bounce back easily from failures.

Being resilient does NOT eliminate the stress that may go along with failure. What it does is give you the strength to tackle your problems head on, and continue to move forward.

The question right now is how can YOU build the resilience to successfully handle so-called failures along the way to your desired goal?

BUILD YOUR RESILIENCE

In spite of what some people think, evidence from scientific research indicates that resilience is not something you're born with. It is a learned "personal strength trait."

How do people become resilient? Actually it's their attitude toward failure that makes them resilient and brings them success. The personal trait of resilience is built over time by dealing in a positive manner with "failure" experiences. Instead of giving up when they hit a bump in the road, people who develop resilience focus on learning what did not work, adjusting their strategy, and pressing on.

The following are some proven-effective methods you can use to build your own resilience:

1. Believe in Your Potential. Research proves that self-belief is important in recovering from difficult events like a failure to achieve something. It's odd how we often tend to overlook our own natural strengths simply because they are natural, and may therefore seem less important.

One good way to build confidence in your own potential is to remind yourself of your natural strengths.

2. Embrace Change. Flexibility is an essential part of resilience. By learning how to be more adaptable, you'll be far better equipped to respond when faced with a failure. While some people tend to be thrown off balance or even crushed by abrupt changes, resilient individuals are able to adapt and thrive.

Create a new habit of viewing yourself as flexible and totally willing to change. Remember, your thoughts truly DO create your reality!

3. Build Problem-Solving Skills. Research shows that people who are able come up with solutions to a problem are better able to cope with failures and setbacks.

Experiment with different strategies to work through common problems. Make it a game – practice building your problem-solving skills, and you'll be far better prepared to cope with any so-called failures.

4. Take Action. Don't just wait for a problem to go away on its own, or sit on the fence waiting for a solution to appear. This just creates discouragement. Analyze your situation, select what you feel is the most promising solution, and put it to work.

There is great power in action. Even if the approach you select is not the perfect answer, at least you'll eliminate something that does not work. Be resilient, and recognize that you have moved one step closer to a solution and the success you desire.

OVERCOME FEAR OF FAILURE

In regard to *past* failure, here's something to think about: The minute you recall a past failure in the present moment, it takes control of both your present *and* your future. Remember that the next time you catch yourself thinking about a past painful memory!

A better response is to just remind yourself that anything in your past made you stronger. You did survive those things after all – or you would not be here today!

A definite sign you might be too focused on the past is if certain situations always trigger the same out-of-control emotional reaction. Many of us just fly off emotionally if an old pain button is pushed.

You might break into a cold sweat and lose your voice at the mere thought of challenging your superior at work even though they're taking advantage of you. Or you may fly into a rage if someone questions your ability to complete even the most insignificant task.

Chances are, all of your logic-based attempts to change such automatic reactions have failed. That's because old memories like these cannot be accessed or controlled using logic.

The fact is, you can only influence these automatic negative reactions using the same power that created them in the first place – emotional power. It takes focused, passionate desire to get past painful memories out of your way.

What follows are some steps you can take to help neutralize the influence of painful past events:

Reclaim your Power. Remember to remind yourself that the past IS past. You do not have to deny any unfortunate or painful things that have happened to you. BUT why would you choose to re-create and re-experience them in the present? You have ALREADY survived those challenges and come out on top. Release them.

Forgive and Move On. The minute you blame something or something for your problems or challenges – you throw your own power away. Release your habit of blaming anyone (including yourself) for any current OR past frustrations, failures, or unhappiness.

Blame just prevents you from moving forward and findings solutions to your challenges. You can kick a dead horse until you break your foot, but it still won't get up and pull your cart down the street.

Remind yourself that your emotional self ONLY learns by making mistakes. Mistakes are part of our natural learning process.

No mistakes equals zero personal growth. And zero personal growth equals more of the same in your life.

Stop Looking Over Your Shoulder. You'll never rise above your past as long as you compare your present situation and challenges to the past. Actually that is a great way to be sure you repeat the same old mistake.

Choose to focus on how you want your life to be right now and in the future. Keep your eye on the road, instead of on the rear view mirror.

Re-Create Your Past. The past truly only influences you today if you choose to re-create it in the present moment. Consider this: All of your memories are actually based on your interpretation of what happened to you. The scientific evidence is that our interpretations often do not necessarily truly reflect what actually occurred.

Dr. Jill Ammon-Wexler

ELEVEN. PUT IT TO WORK

So what do you really want to have in your life? What kind of a home? What car? How much money do you want? What kind of relationship or friends? What does your IDEAL lifestyle look like?

Life rewards action. No matter how great you at dreaming or visualizing, dreams only come true when you wake up and go to work. When you really want to get something done and done right, there's really only one choice. That choice is to ACT.

What is the one thing you want more than anything? You're poised on the starting line waiting for the signal. When will the starting gun fire? You will hear that motivating "bang" when you choose to take action!

Will you feel totally confident of success at that moment? Probably not. But the importance of that moment is that you feel you're ready to take a calculated risk to achieve a goal you passionately desire.

One. See yourself as big enough to stand in the face of any mistakes and the consequences. Remember, even a failed attempt at something is an indication you are stretching yourself.

Two. Aim for your best, but be realistic. Better than seeking absolute perfection, simply strive to make bold decisions. You now know how to interpret what most people call failure, and realize it is just a step forward on the path to your success.

Three. Focus on having actually ALREADY achieved your desired end result no matter what is thrown at you. Really picture being there NOW!

Four. We never know how long it may take to achieve a Law of Attraction goal, or what lessons we will have to learn along the way. Be patient. Enjoy pursuing your dreams, and know that fear of failure no longer controls your decisions, and you will achieve your goals.

Five. One of the most important things you can do is to set up and follow a DAILY success practice. Keep yourself on track and on purpose.

Dr. Jill Ammon-Wexler

TWELVE. MORE RESOURCES

A Great Next Step... Are you SERIOUS about getting your Law of Attraction goals moving FAST? The author is a world renowned psychologist and 45-year pioneer in brain/mind research. Dr. Ammon-Wexler has helped people from around the world achieve higher states of awareness Dr. Jill's unique "LAW OF ATTRACTION SUCCESS: Create Future Memories" unique collection of downloadable MP3 special brainwave trainings will help reset your beliefs and intentions to bring faster LOA success. This special collection of stereo-quality MP3s is valued at $69.75, but is only $19.95 for you as a book buyer.

http://QuantumLeapAudios.com/future-memories/

Are YOU Ready to Go Deeper? Are **YOU** one of those special people with a passionate desire to accomplish more in your life? If so, Dr. Ammon-Wexler would like to personally invite you to come participate in her unique **QUANTUM MIND TRAINING PROGRAM**.

Develop and refine your brain/mind power in the comfort of your own home. This exciting 3-month online program is packed with unique training audios, videos, and specially engineered brainwave training.

The end results include greatly increased creativity, focus, intelligence, total stress management, mental clarity, and remarkably superior levels of brain/mind performance. Open up your natural genius and tap into higher, more valuable states of awareness and consciousness. Go learn more and take advantage of a temporary book buyer's discount=>

http://www.HotBrainz.com

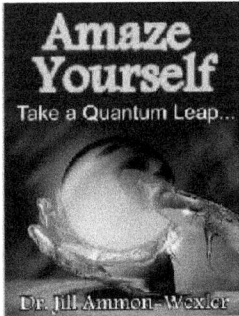

We have many more printed books, ebooks, audio books, brainwave training collections, and special training programs. Come read some interesting articles and browse through our collection=>

http://www.BuildMindPower.com

Dr. Jill Ammon-Wexler

ABOUT THE AUTHOR

The Author, Jill Ammon-Wexler is doctor of psychology and 45-year pioneer brain/mind researcher. She is also a "life adventurer" with a passion for finding, and then pushing beyond, her personal "limits." She has pursued higher states of consciousness since her late teen years, first climbed a mountain alone at age 16, and then had to find her way down the mountain in a wild snow storm.

During her university years she studied with amazing leaders like Fritz Perls, Virginia Satir, Soygal Rinpoche and Alan Watts. She also walked on fire, did sweat lodges, studied with shamanic elders, and become the holder of a coyote talking stick.

After receiving her Masters degree in psychology, she shaved her head and spent 6 months in a monastic Buddhist retreat. She then completed a PhD in psychology, became a clinical hypnotherapist and certified clinical biofeedback provider, and began her professional career as a pioneer mind power trainer and personal transformation coach.

Over the years Dr. Jill has also provided mind power training for organizations and individuals from around the world. She has traveled through several countries on her continuing search for yet more wisdom and adventure. Information about Dr. Jill's other mind-expanding books and training programs can be found at=> **http://www.buildmindpower.com**

www.ingramcontent.com/pod-product-compliance
Lightning Source LLC
Chambersburg PA
CBHW061745020426
42331CB00006B/1361

9 780099 103793